To Libb

ALBORADA (DAWN)

A Cross-Cultural Memoir in Poetry

Wishing you many happy
dawns!

[signature]

ALBORADA (DAWN)

A Cross-Cultural Memoir in Poetry

Nylda Dieppa

Published by Orange Blossom Publishing
2020 Geronimo Trail
Maitland, Florida 32751
www.OrangeBlossomBooks.com

Second edition print ISBN: 978-1-949935-73-8
Second edition ebook ISBN: 978-1-949935-74-5
Second edition Library of Congress Control Number: 2023906831

Second edition author photo by Nylda Beatriz Photography
Second edition cover artwork by Sanja Mosic
Second edition interior formatting by Autumn Skye

The first edition of Alborada: A Poetic Memoir Across Cultures, © 2014 by Nylda Dieppa, was published in 2014 by Little Pond Publishing, Satellite Beach, Florida.

First edition ISBN 978-1-940720-07-4
First edition Library of Congress Control Number 2014933884

First edition cover design by Misfit Creative (https://TinyURL.com/misfitcreative, formerly najcreatives at www.NAJCreatives.com)
Cover Artwork: Nylda Dieppa (www.NyldaDieppa.com)

Printed in the United States of America
Maitland, Florida

PRAISE FOR ALBORADA (DAWN)

"Nylda Dieppa is a woman of triumph. Her poems are real, honest, spirited, and may tell as much of your story as her own. I love her redemptive spirit."
—Tama Kieves, best-selling author of *Inspired & Unstoppable: Wildly Succeeding in Your Life's Work!*

"Dieppa writes from the heart; her poems tell her story without pretension. A beautiful work, uncovering a beautiful person."

—T. K. Thorne, author of the award-winning *Noah's Wife*, *Last Chance for Justice: How Relentless Investigators Uncovered New Evidence Convicting the Birmingham Church Bombers*, and many other books

"The works here show an incredible amount of talent. The cultural connotation of the work was well done and consistent. . . . Artistically, 'Damn Free' showed a lot of energy and a feistiness that I appreciated."

—Tony Burnett, award-winning poet and songwriter

"*Alborada* is . . . a document of sorrow and healing throughout a woman's life. Paradoxically, there is joy—in family, music, and Nature. . . . [In] 'Sheet Music' . . . concrete imagery paints a vivid picture of a child, her people, and heritage all coming together over music. Piano lessons are ordinary, but this poem renders them extraordinary. Memorable!"

—Sylvia Riojas Vaughn, poet whose "Tres Vestidos de las Muertas" was nominated for the 2013 Pushcart Awards by *Red River Review*

"I love the Latin flavor and the love that shines out. . . . I think this book would appeal to all women. So many have experienced the same pains and insights."

—Alice Friedman, poet and author of *What Now, Courage?*

"Fabulous idea to tell a story through poetry. It compelled me to keep turning the page to the next poem. I read the first 20 pages and then finished the rest in one sitting."

—Susan Gurnik, writer

"Your poems are so palpable, and have a vulnerability that allows people to deeply connect with them. I truly enjoyed them! There must be a Spanish version."

—Coralis Solomon, MSCP

"How fortunate am I to read your holy truths! Brava! . . . I love your work. . . . I'll be reading your poems at bedtime so I can sleep and reflect on them."

—Juliana Aragón Fatula, author of
Red Canyon Falling on Churches

"Clearly, your heart is wide open in many of these autobiographical poems, and I love that. You've got determination and style . . . I admire you, Nylda, for your compassion and your willingness to speak your heart so freely."

—Charlene Edge, author of *Undertow: My Escape from the Fundamentalism and Cult Control of The Way International* and *From the Porch to the Page: A Guidebook for the Writing Life*

"The author has a depth of feeling and is unafraid to explore pain."

—Ken Pelham, author of *Out of Sight, Out of Mind: A Writer's Guide to Mastering Viewpoint* (RPLA's 2015 Published Book of the Year) and multiple titles in other genres

"Despite all the pain in your life, you face the future with hope. . . . Your author's note . . . gives readers just enough background to enter the poems more easily and also gives them a reason to trust you. . . . 'Vacation' is my favorite poem—absolutely devastating! I think everybody will read it with their heart in their throat."

—Lynn Schiffhorst, multi-award-winning poet and author

"In Alborada, Nylda opens her heart to her readers, inviting them on a poetic journey that makes her life art. If only we could all recall our key moments with such vivid imagery! Readers will learn about the author's life, and by sharing those experiences, readers will learn more about themselves. The book is by turns, funny, sad, touching, and uplifting, and shares not only stories of survival, but also love and hope. Alborada makes readers feel the way a great work of art should."

Peter M. Gordon
President, Florida State Poets Association, Orlando Area Poets

Dedication

To my abuelo, Luis Rodríguez Boneta, the first poet I admired. It's a shame I don't remember ever sitting in your lap. And to Mami, Carmen Angélica Rodríguez, who taught me to love and respect you.

To my dear Papi, Jorge J. Dieppa, who showed me a bit of his creativity and insisted I develop mine.

TABLE OF CONTENTS

AUTHOR'S NOTE

*A*lborada (*Dawn*) is a book forty-plus years in the making. Although many of these poems were inspired by dark times over the years since I started writing as a youth, others have arisen from the renewal of my energy and inspiration as night has turned into day. New insights have emerged as I have begun to experience life afresh from a maturity born of experience. The personal growth process is ongoing.

Some readers have wondered why I stayed so long in an unhappy marriage. My ex-husband and I were children when we started dating and baby adults when we married. Cultural mores, immaturity, and the stresses of life brought us to a point where love was not enough to keep us happy together, but I still felt it was my duty to remain faithful to my vows "till death do us part."

One day I realized that I had died to myself, and my future depended on starting a new life. I confronted the fact of my unsound marriage—and grieved my lost dreams for many years. The passage of time and the perspective and personal growth achieved by confronting unavoidable realities have brought me a measure of healing and kept us on friendly terms.

I want to mention that a broken heart remains scarred forever, yet a happy and fulfilled life is possible when you do the difficult work of facing your fears and letting resentments go. It's a roller-coaster journey, not a simple stroll along the beach. Faith and courage have gone a long way toward helping me see the light of a new day. There is no easy way out of broken dreams, and these poems reflect that. I hope they keep you company on your journey from midnight to dawn.

About culture clash: "Always in My Heart" may lead you to experience culture clash—and I hope it does. It is in part an ode to Puerto Rican poet and musician Noel Estrada and his universally loved song "En mi Viejo San Juan" ("In My Old San Juan.") I have added descriptors to some names in order to help those who are not familiar with Puerto Rican landmarks and kept the discordant (to some ears) last stanza to honor the roots I celebrate. It may dilute the technical quality of the poem, but it makes my point.

An item of style: You may notice a liberal use of exclamation points. This is a deliberate decision to convey the strength and passion of a Puerto Rican woman's voice. In Spanish, it is perfectly acceptable to use three or four exclamation points, and my critique group friends called me their exclamation point queen!!!!

I love to get feedback from my readers. Please write to me at info@ nyldadieppa.com. I will enjoy hearing what you have to say.

NOTE TO THE SECOND EDITION

I am thrilled to have my award-winning book back in print in a beautiful new edition packed with new poems, a new title, and a lovely new cover. It took me a while to say goodbye to the original design of the book cover because—you know—it is both exciting and wistful to see your first baby grow up!

Alborada (Dawn): A Cross-Cultural Memoir in Poetry is a story of survival and rebirth after confronting the storms I have faced throughout my life. On this book's cover, I want to illustrate the idea of surviving personal onslaughts and celebrating a new dawn. I also try to project an image of memories forged through the clash of two cultures, and I want to avoid potential misunderstandings or conflicts among my readers by explaining why and how I chose the new book cover that means so much to me.

You might think Americans are passionate about their political affiliations, but that may be a recent historical development. (I am a poet, not a historian!) When I first moved to the United States forty-five years ago, I was shocked by the relative apathy of those who had the right to vote in general elections. According to official counts reported by the United States Census Bureau, "only 54 percent of the voting age population (18 years old and over) voted in the 1980 Presidential election" in the U.S.[1] In the same year, in contrast, registered voter turnout in Puerto Rico was 88.3%![2]

---

[1]   "Voting and Registration in the Election of November 1982," Census.gov Resource Library, United States Census Bureau, page last revised October 8, 2021, https://www.census.gov/library/publications/1982/demo/p20-370.html.

[2]   "1980 Puerto Rican general election," Wikipedia: The Free Encyclopedia, Wikimedia Foundation Inc., last edited 27 March 2023, 07:38 (UTC), https://en.wikipedia.org/wiki/1980_Puerto_Rican_general_election.

Growing up in Puerto Rico, political debates were a national pastime. Three principal parties had developed by the time I started paying attention: the Partido Popular Democrático (PPD), symbolized by a red *pava*, the hand-woven straw hat traditionally worn by *campesinos*; the Partido Nuevo Progresista (PNP), whose symbol is a bright blue palm tree; and the Partido Independentista Puertorriqueño (PIP), which flaunted the Puerto Rican flag at a time when the US had made it illegal to do so, with a green-and-white banner as its logo. As the last name implies, the PIP strives toward independence from the United States for the island; the PNP wants Puerto Rico to become a full-fledged state of the union; the PPD supports the status quo as a free, associated state.

All of us proclaim pride in our flag.

Puerto Ricans on the island archipelago and in the diaspora suffer, each in their own way, from a colonially imposed identity crisis. With traditional Boricua passion, most people showed their party affiliation as I was growing up by proudly showing the appropriate symbol, wearing "their color" everywhere, and even painting their homes in the proper accent color! Twelve months a year, fiery debates flared, and too often families and friendships were devastated (as is currently happening in the US).

One of the book cover designs I considered had a fortress wall with a sentry box (a *garita*), suggesting the solidity and permanence of El Morro Castle through the centuries, but it is such an overused image when referring to Puerto Rico that it felt like a tourist advertisement. The twisted palm tree I chose instead says to me, "I withstood many hurricanes, and I am standing firm here." The Puerto Rican flag proclaims the personal identity that gives me the foundation to survive. I am sure there will be those who demand I add a pava to the design so no party is left out. That would be for another type of book, for someone else to write.

These symbols can be interpreted in various ways. Some readers may think my book cover is making a political statement. I hope the dual language title helps point out this is the private story of a Puerto Rican woman in the diaspora and not a political declaration. It is the articulation of my own experiences for the encouragement, inspiration, and entertainment of others. I think this cover illustration achieves my purpose.

This book comes out at what we all hope will be the tail end of the COVID-19 pandemic. The lessons I learned through the years portrayed here have helped me understand that—even during the dark days of innumerable deaths and suffering—as we prayed a cure could be found for this terrible disease, deep down inside us, the knowledge of a bright new day to come could support us through this unimaginable journey. Although we will need to live with the coronavirus for the foreseeable future, those clouds will dissipate as new strides are made in the prevention and treatment of the disease.

I hope my old readers enjoy the new offerings and my new readers discover an experience that enriches their lives and broadens their horizons. It is a blessing to see how the new poems included here—previously lost in the morass of my old hard drives, misfiled papers, and disintegrating napkins—are enhancing the depth and quality of this book as they, too, finally get to see the light of day.

DESPERTAR
(AWAKENING)

TRIGGER WARNING

I wrote and I wrote and I wrote
to tell an old story.
MY story.
My own damned personal story.

I don't know how I was able to tell it
but I had to—because my story
would come out
whether I wanted it to or not.

I WARN YOU:
You WILL be triggered
if I did my job right,
if I opened my heart truly
to you, my reader.

My work may make you cry,
have a panic attack,
anger you to an extreme,
leave you trembling with raw emotion.

And that means I used the right words
to reach the (dark) pits of your heart—passions
you probably didn't know
until today were lurking there.

Please forgive me
if you become   discombobulated.
I didn't write to make you feel that way.
I did because I had to

to be true to myself
and my own terrible depths.

May my words help you
discover your own.

A SECRET MESSAGE

Shhh! Come here.

Sit on my lap and listen
to the story of your *abuelita*,
your Awa, when she was little.

She was smart and pretty.
She was talented and artsy.
She could do lots of things,
and she was sweet and nice and helpful.

And when she grew up, she met a boy
who was handsome and charming
and played the guitar
and serenaded her.

But she stopped believing in herself
and thought she couldn't live without him,
so she stopped living
while she was married to him.

And then she had to admit
he didn't love her,
perhaps never had,
and had to learn to live for herself.

The End

Shhh! *The Beginning*

LOVE POEM

Write me a love poem, you say.
A love poem?
Is there any other kind?

There must be love somewhere
in order to write a poem
full of emotion and insight.

To touch someone's soul
with words that are full of anguish
or pleasure, pride, or joy.

Why would I put two words together
if I had nothing to say
about my soul or yours or ours?

Why would you linger on them,
tasting the terror, watching the wind,
hearing the hope, memorizing the music

if there was no love in them
to touch your heart
with my soul's blood?

REINITA

The first time I saw the little bird
with the yellow chest and black wings
she was almost at my eye level
pecking at crumbs on the balcony wall.
I remember the blue sky

hidden behind the vine that grows
on the wrought iron and blooms
a profusion of paper-thin purples.
My two little brothers in diapers

and me freshly out of mine,
our mother inside the house
caring for her paralyzed mother.
My brothers played in the shade,

the *reinita* performed her task as she sang,
a sweet perfume surrounding me
as I kept the younger ones safe for a while.

GROWTH SONG

I remember growing, changing.
Joy, hurt, chaos.

Old aunts in balcony rocking chairs,
praying the rosary.
Watching.
Mumbling blessings and curses.
Children playing, running, stumbling.

Me, sitting on the sidewalk fence,
singing songs.
Passersby stop, greet me, listen.
I sing, sing, sing all songs:
Old. New. Baby. Grown-up.

A checkers-cheating cousin laughs,
taunting me:
"Baby, baby, baby songs."
Cars, buses, taxis, trucks drive by.

Tears drop, anger builds.
Only singing heals my hurt.

FIRST CRUSH

What does a nine-year-old girl know
about grown-up love or hormones?
She doesn't recognize her body
with its shaking knees,
sweating palms,
crazy heartbeats.

She only understands
(as she trembles in her ignorance
and revels in the excitement)
like facing a precipice—

that this sweet, handsome older man
who wouldn't hurt a fly
makes her stomach somersault
as they sit together in the dark theater.

BINOCULAR

From a distance
you were gruff, rough,
and outright rude.
Up close you were sweet and soft,
cuddly and warm,
funny and smart.

From a distance
you were short-tempered
and loud, quick to judge,
and very demanding.
Up close I saw your high standards,
your sense of justice and equality,
and your generosity of spirit.

From a distance
you did not pay attention
to your bottom line and were up to here
with credit card bills.
Up close, though,
you were generous to a fault
and made sure we always had
the best AMEX could buy.

From a distance
you were unbending,
resentful, unforgiving,
stingy with compliments
and endearments.
Up close you were witty and passionate,
loyal and honest,
and loved people through and through.

We were close at the beginning
and at the end.
In the middle
we were good friends.
You wiped my butt at two days old,
and I wiped yours at eighty-two.

You taught me how to bake orange cake
out of the first box ever sold,
to love art, shade my carbon sketches
after paying attention to the light,
the dignity of all creatures,
and how important it was
for a woman to think
and have a college degree.

At the beginning
you called my boyfriend "the enemy,"
even as you chaperoned us
everywhere we wanted to go,
but in the end
he was your beloved son.

At the end
it took you a while
to change your focus
and stop asking me why I was "so good to you,"
and to remember the loving care
you gave Mami's mami
when she couldn't care for herself.
And although you never said so,
I knew you forgave her
for not liking you
at the beginning
because you were not baptized a Catholic.

When things started to look different
and the trivial was important no more,
you told me you loved me
over and over and over.
You said I was good and you were proud of me
and it was OK for me to rule your life
as long as I did it gently
and allowed you to live
until you died.

At the beginning
you held me in your arms,
feeding me from a bottle
before it was fashionable to do so,
while you smoked and studied
for your PhD.

At the end
you could barely hold
your great-granddaughter in your lap,
but it gave you great joy
to look into her innocent eyes
and see yourself in them.

At the end
you were disappointed
not to receive Communion,
and I held you as you took
three long deep gulps of air
and left me an orphan
with a great tolerance for ambiguity.

And we both knew
In the deepest recesses of our souls
that we loved each other enough
to say goodbye.

LINEAGE

Three women fearing the Lord:
Abuela in a wooden wheelchair,
Mami in her personal prayer room,
me in my hidden home office.

Abuela, giving up walking
(to save my mother's life)
and fixing broken toys for poor children
as she repaid her promise to God.

Mami, praying for the redemption of humanity
and the forgiveness of her own sins,
worrying about her loved ones' salvation because
her God was a god of justice.

Me, studying and going on medical missions,
serving my family, fighting domestic violence,
crying for lost chances and unused talents
as I waited for God to remember me.

Strong in our weaknesses,
giving glory to God,
paralyzed by fear,
united in love.

NANILEILOE

Who are you, precious child?
Where did you come from
to bring us joy and laughter
when we needed it most?

The first time I saw your big brown eyes
was not when they were still green
but when your mother was born,
my very first child and purest love.

They were just as bright and intelligent
and when I saw myself in them
my heart took a leap
and I was certain there was a God.

Many years have passed,
and my baby's beautiful eyes have dulled.
I see more tears in them
than bright ideas and happy thoughts.

I couldn't protect her, though I tried,
and now I look at you,
beautiful and perfect child,
my pride and joy,

and remind myself to forgive me
so your mother may do the same
when we both discover
we couldn't protect you either.

THE ELEMENT

¡Qué elemento! my old aunt used to say
when a sharp-looking dandy
walked by her balcony
as she sat in her rocking chair
praying and cursing a storm.

What an element! What a subject!
What an item! What a creature!
There's no translation good enough
because the sarcasm in her voice
belied the true emotions in her heart.

¡Qué elemento! my aunt used to say
while watching TV or reading the news
about a wise guy who outsmarted the system
and came out looking squeaky clean.
There was envy in her voice.

¡Qué elemento! she would add sometimes
when sharing a story of the no-good husband
who hit his wife daily, abused his children,
and robbed his boss after morning Mass.
I could tell she would have hit him, if she could.

MEMORIES OF A PORTRAIT EN PLEIN AIR

"Memories of a Portrait en Plein Air" debuted in a public reading at the Albin Polasek Museum & Sculpture Gardens on April 27, 2018.

Twenty-five years and the dust of life
have faded the memory of this happy family.
All seven or eight of them
are assembled together around the big bench
by the pool you cannot see.
You know it's there
by the chlorine smell still catching
in their nostrils, all these years past,
while the lush, dark green foliage
of the philodendron behind those posing,
whispers in the warm Florida breeze.

Your eyes land first on the fluffy white dog
with big black eyes and silly overbite.
He seems to smile, content
on the lap of a lovely young girl
with bouncy brown curls and radiant red lips:
the middle child, mostly a woman now.
Solid, relaxed, confident—
the windows of her soul open slits of sparkle
above her wide smile.

The children appear to be quite grown,
except the nine-year-old,
who sits demurely in the shade
amid her brother and sisters,
fingers gently interlaced on her lap.
She stares at the camera directly.
With a self-satisfied Mona Lisa smile,
she claims she knows exactly what's going on.
But you don't think so.

The young man pictured at the bottom left
is the second-oldest of the siblings.
He sports a candid smile of accomplishment
since he just set the camera's timer
and smartly rushed to his place

without mussing his thick black hair,
his long-sleeved sapphire shirt,
or the tie that imitates
the one his father tore off his own neck
not ten minutes ago,
as he rushed in from work.

Behind and between the baby and the big brother
sits the eldest daughter,
an enchanting Middle Eastern–looking presence
with the haunting dark eyes of an old secret
and her mother's lovely smile.
Hardly home for a college break,
she pulls her knee to her chest,
sure she won't share what she's learned there.

Barely out of childhood into adolescence,
the fourth child shyly peeks out
from behind her older siblings,
her school-girl woes tossed aside.
For a second, she revels in the joy of the moment—
all of them together in bright daylight.
All of them sharing the same foolish mirth.
And the mother close to her
the happiest and proudest of all.

Still in her young womanhood,
she reaches out to encircle this beautiful brood
she has produced and shaped,
and it's almost magical how she glows
as she stands in front of her husband,
who may or may not be pinching her butt,
as if she needed any help to grin tonight.

He leans close to his wife to make sure
there's still room in the picture for him
and he goofily grins as he slants
into this lovely, beloved assembly of souls,

his unconstrained hand tense,
expecting the inescapable call
of the beeper on his belt
to bully him yet again toward his one true love.

The grinning white dog still lies quietly,
confident of his central place in this grouping.

La Luz del Día
(Daylight)

ANOTHER NAME FOR DEDICATION

Busy, busy,
not a minute to spare.
She goes from chore to chore, task to task, without rest.
"What a way to feel useful and needed!"
She chuckles to herself
as she moves on to the next undertaking
with lightning speed.
Without her sense of humor
she would be crazy by now.

She is obsessed with efficiency.
She crams her personal planner,
a cute little thing of a lesser-known brand
that she bought at a great discount price,
with hour-by-hour appointments.
She stays up all hours of the night (or morning)
reading, writing, getting all set,
or relaxing with a quick card game or ten.

She reads while she works out,
she prays while she drives,
she listens to the news while she brushes her teeth
and while she cooks dinner.

Then one day a man gives her a big bear hug
and her eyes are opened.
A solitary tear rolls down her cheek
as she returns to hot sync her organizer.

SHEET MUSIC

Notes on a staff,
        like blackbirds
                on electric lines
                        or clotheslines,

bring me back
        to my childhood
                and a time
                        when life was sweet
                                and fresh.

I started
        reading the big fat
                round notes
        and graduated little by little
to Clementi
        and Hanon   and Czerny
                and Beethoven's "Für Elise,"
                        Oh, so sweet!

I worked hard
                on a daily basis,
        sometimes two   or three hours a day
                and conquered
        the Puerto Rican *danza*,
                "*Mis Amores*,"
        and the one titled
                "*Violeta*"
                        like my neighbor.

And I played   four-hand duets
with my mother   who was too
shy to play   anything else
and sat   for hours
listening to   Olga
who used to   be
my mom's   good friend
and now   my teacher
playing   the piano.

NYLDA DIEPPA

I can't believe I'd forgotten her name when her
face and fingers were so clear in my heart and the
metronome clicking and me yawning
                    as I did the *solfeggio*
                                    one-two-three.

And I improved   so much
                        in my performance

that I could play the
quintuple
        chords
                that look
                    like
                        little specks
                                on a strand
                                        of hair

and the M e L o D i O u S
                tremolos
        That   f l u t t e r   so.

Yet—
I didn't believe
                in myself
                and my talent
and I stopped
        playing my
        beloved

(Sheet!)
        music.

ON HOW I
WANT TO WRITE

Don't teach me how to write.
I don't want any formulas.
My words should be strong and tasty,
appealing to all my senses
like the aroma and flavor
of fresh-baked Tigua bread.

Oh, the warm satisfaction,
the fulfillment and excitement of my whole body
after wrenching life-giving substance
from that simple, unassuming meal!

And don't look over my shoulder, either,
when I'm writing,
for the nakedness of my feelings is embarrassing.
Better to wait until I have decently clothed them
in the proper words that show off my beauty
without indecently exposing me.

In Love Again

Time stopped for nine months
while I waited.
And it stopped again while I labored.
I took deep breaths,
concentrated on my child,
and managed the pain like an expert.

My husband was finally at my side
(after three or four deliveries
mostly without him).
This time he knew the routine
and he was all there,
rubbing my back, coaching me.

My previous delivery took nine minutes—
the taxicab baby girl.
But this time the clock kept ticking
and the hours slipping by,
and me riding the pain
like the authority I was.

Seven unnecessary hours later
the obstetrician learned he was wrong
in abandoning me as I labored
(since I had a great nurse and helpful husband).
My baby needed help
to finish her trip into this world.

The next day when I held her in my arms
I was livid at the lazy scoundrel
for scratching her skull five times—
and almost killing her.

But when I looked into her deep, dark eyes,
I fell in love once more (and forgot him)
and wondered how such beauty and perfection
had been delivered to me.

SOMETHING SWEET

There is nothing sweeter than a young child,
big round eyes gazing in amazement
at the world,
seeing things I've never seen before
or appreciated.

Most of my life I've been surrounded by babies,
little children, big kids, young adults.
As they get older
they lose some of their original sweetness
and become richer, more complex.
An acquired taste.

REALIZATION

There was a time I thought
I had a limited number of words
in my head and I was afraid
to put them down
on paper
stingily believing
if I did
I would quickly run out of them

But in the last twenty-five days
I've typed in 48,687
and still have
plenty more
to go

IMPOSSIBLES

I dream impossibles.
What merit may there be
in dreaming countless verses
that ne'er the light will see?

Or dreaming all those pictures
so delicate to feel
in watercolors varied
of orchids, pinks, or teals?

Oh, the grand creations,
the magnificent indulgence,
the breathtaking exhilaration
of gloriously revealed wonders!

Will fanciful chimeras evermore
cling as captives of my soul,
shackled and buried in a deep, dark cave,
confronted with my prison door?

FLYING HIGH

My own prisoner I am
of dreams impossible,
of pain untold,
of work interminable,
of love unsolved.

I strive for freedom
yet I fear
the dizziness, the altitude,
of flying on a string.

WISHES IN THE WIND

I wish these bright, breezy days
would last forever
to blow away the anguish
of Uncertainty
Fear
Grief
Anger

I wish I had the answers to
Why
Who
When
How

I wish I could hug you
and kiss you
and whisper in your ear:
I love you.
We're safe!

REALIZATION II

Childhood love—thought eternal—
faced life's wrong turns with coldness infernal.
Broken vows, brutal betrayals,
long waits,
drawn-out hopes,
passionate reconciliations kept afloat
by practiced lies perpetual.

What honest heritage would I restore
with sweet, unaware self-deception
that built scornful castles in air—
dark dungeons for my detention?

Why wait for the prodigal prince
who swore eternal love and protection?

ATARDECER
(DUSK)

TO THE YOUNG WOMAN IN THE OLD PHOTO

Why are you so forlorn, dear,
restrained, despairing?

Your beautiful dress and jewelry
show you live a comfortable life

but your eyes and half smile
hide your secrets.

Is it not enough for you
to have what you need to bloom?

Are you looking for more,
hoping, yearning,

or waiting at your doorstep
for your lover's kiss

that is way overdue?

46

EXPLORATION

A path opens before me
in the middle of the night.
It's a dirt road canopied by luscious trees.
Further ahead, a fork.

Where do I turn?
Does it really matter
if there's abundance everywhere?
I could go this way
and find fame and fortune
or I could go that way
and find unending love.

But if my heart is truly open
to the goodness of the Universe
I can find love in one
and recognition and security in the other

because I am one with the two roads
and the future is all within me.

ALWAYS IN MY HEART

"Always in My Heart" was written in praise of "En mi Viejo San Juan" by Noel Estrada.

July 4, 1979, I left my island
for a new life
in this big, strange country
that I thought I knew so well
without hope or promise
of a new and improved life
or a better love.

Alone, I lugged my three kids,
one of them in a straw basket,
the other two tied to my waist
so I wouldn't lose them
through two airports,
two airplanes,
a mass of luggage.

Yes, I brought a lot of baggage with me
but I left my heart behind
floating in the warm waves of Luquillo beach,
behind the thick walls of El Morro castle,
in the moist, pungent earth of El Yunque forest.

My family grew to seven
with a kid born in Georgia
and another in Texas.
Then we ended up in Florida
where my parents died
and I felt lost
without the mountains at my back
and the seashore so far away.

Like yesterday's poet sang,
"My hair has turned white
and destiny has made fun
of my terrible nostalgia."
And though I have been back
"to the San Juan that I loved,"
I am who I am because of my *patria*.

DAMN FREE

Nothing like living in a free country
where we are our own masters
and can choose what to wear,
what to eat, who to marry.

Nothing like the freedom
of choosing the work we do,
the songs we sing,
the guns we carry.

We're free to say what we want,
sleep around with whomever
falls in our bed tonight,
and free to leave them tomorrow.

Free to be ourselves,
to think of no one at all,
to be cynical, religious,
to wear heels five inches tall.

It's an obsession, an addiction,
a mass delusion or madness
to keep pushing the boundaries
of this heavy freedom we carry.

A TINY THING MAKES ALL THE DIFFERENCE

It's one thing to write because I *must*
and another to write because I *have* to.
When I *must* write the words fly freely
from my breathless soul
and land exactly
        where they belong.

When I *have to* write, I struggle
to fill the blank page that stares at me
challenging me
to go deep into my heart
and discover on time
        the truth of my longings.

HALFWAY POINT

Thirty-two-thousand words into my novel,
my heroine is about to fall in love.
I have described her happy childhood,
her doting father, her desire for perfection,
how her own life-threatening illness
destroyed her mother by an excess of faith.

I showed her miserable adolescence,
trying to make up for being alive,
her yearning for freedom,
her desire for fun and love and lightness.

She sits in front of the mirror now,
combing her hair and primping
before the *Fiestas Patronales*,
her patron saint's festivities.

She can almost taste the music
and hear the pungent smell of the fritters,
feel the twinkle in the dark brown eyes,
smell the smile under the thin black moustache.

Her world is about to change.
Her prayers will be answered.
She will get married, have children,
run away from her mother's abuse.

But I hate to bring her there,
dressed in her favorite blue cotton dress,
the color of the Virgin's mantle,
because I know she doesn't know
the worst is yet to come.

SLOW SUNSET
IN SARASOTA

Sensations, connections, mind-sets.
Brown and purple and yellow shudders.
Bright yellow, intense,
almost orange-gold circled by fluffy blue-gray
against the dark indigo of the beach sky.

It's dinnertime for the sea birds
and it's fun watching them through tears of envy
soaring, diving, hunting, gulping.
Little white seagulls with black feet tucked under
and the heavy, powerful pelican
whose mouth can hold more
than his belly can.

They teach me perspective
and to dive in at great speeds
hoping for the satisfaction of a primal need fulfilled.
There's something to be said for fearlessness
and speed and light and sea breeze.
Twisted, bundled together in a fast-moving kaleidoscope
of sand, wind, salt, and feathers.

PINEAPPLE FLIGHT

Jumpstart my low energies
with pineapple ice cream
strawberry fields in Oahu.

I am drained of energy
and almost depressed, but not.
More like frustrated
for the slow motion of the churning wheels.

Blue skies and gentle breezes
in a quiet beach shaded by palm trees,
golden sand runs through my fingers
and the salt air kisses my eyelashes.

Glorious escape after a long day giving.

ODE TO THE GRAVID BANANA TREE

Bunches of fat green ape fingers.
huddle around the knobby pole
that ends in a shy cluster of yellow eyelashes
demurely covered in a wine-colored veil,
strong and thick and protective and bruised.

Food for some, decoration for others,
nuisance for the ignorant
but beautiful.
Heavy, delicious *mafafos*,
I waited many years for your gestation.

Many years too I've waited for my own
Birth
Awakening
Empowerment.
The culmination of what I was supposed to become:
beautiful, strong, foreign, pungent, fulfilling
food for friends and foes alike.

Only the wise, the patient, the brave
can look beyond the blood-covered front
that hangs, limp and lifeless-looking,
and picture beauty and sweetness inside.

LOVE SONG IN TWO TEMPOS

How can I pull outside of myself
this anguish of sharing with you who I am,
where I've been,
how life has brought me to my knees?

It's a matter of self-discipline, my mother used to say,
of doing what you must, and doing it right.

But who am I but an open book
for you to pass by and ignore
or worse yet,
read and misinterpret?

It's a matter of self-discipline, my mother used to say,
of having faith and doing what's right.

It is not enough to make myself vulnerable
to your prejudices and your judgment:
I must find what makes you tremble
with my joy and terror, sweat and laughter.

It's a matter of self-discipline, my mother used to say,
"My nerves, I put them in my pocket."

I must recreate for you the sharp scent of the sea breeze
and the soft rustle of the palm fronds
and the insistence of the moist evening song
of the tiny frog that dies away from its homeland
as it piteously chirps: "*Coquí, coquí, coquí.*"

It's a matter of translation, I must say:
"Coh-kee, coh-kee, coh-kee."
A sad, humid love song for my island.

Itoo was supposed to die many years ago
when I left my sunny, windswept paradise
for this strange country with its strange customs,
its busy isolation, and lonely independence.

But I put my grief in my pocket
and dutifully housewifed a large family.

Yet something in me was strong, young, beautiful—
and it kept me alive when I should have died
sad and lonely with the pain that strangles the throat
when the beach is too far to touch,
the fragrant rainforest only a faint dream.

It's a matter of self-discipline, my mother used to say.
So I hid my grief in my pocket.

What keeps you alive, my dear friend,
and smelling sweet and singing?
What foreign-tasting country
do you inhabit and survive in?

What's inside that gives us courage
to live in spite of life itself?
Mami, Mami, Mami.

NOCHE
(NIGHT)

ABOUT LIFE

Bright, balmy days befall us
created for waves and sand and searching
for roses and avocado trees
and broad beams on kids' faces.

Other days droop dark and dreary,
cold, taunting and tormenting,
and all they seem to be good for
is crawling under a cover and crying.

PRUDENCE

Prudence is an old word,
the name of a virtue,
one of my mother's favorites.

She was prudent to a fault,
biting her tongue,
looking the other way.

She took action
for the sake of prudence—
and sometimes she didn't.

A week before my wedding
Mami answered a phone call
from my fiancé's girlfriend
who said she was pregnant.

Mami didn't say a word to me.

She confronted him
and chose to believe it was a lie.
And I never heard about it.

Now, five children later,
five lovers later,
one divorce later,

I wonder what would've happened
to my shattered life
if she had said something.

NUERA

It wasn't easy being my father-in-law's *nuera*
because in the back of his mind
I wasn't simply his daughter-in-law
but another woman
to lord it over and to bully.

VACATION

She's barely seventeen,
my baby,
the little doll I played with
only a few years ago.
I kissed her tiny baby feet
that smelled so sweet
and her wee hands caressed my breast
as she gorged herself with warm milk.

She and I were one once
a little while ago
but gradually she grew up,
beginning to blossom,
a beautiful young woman
full of passion and conviction.
Much like me in very many ways
yet so much her own person.

Tonight I ride behind the ambulance,
in her father's blue Volvo
that I borrowed two days ago
to drive up to the beach with her, my baby,
so the two of us could spend time together
reacquainting ourselves with each other
since I had to put my foot down
at her teenage defiance.

I called these men to rescue her tonight,
a very difficult thing for me.
I wanted to take care of her myself
not have to depend on strangers,
but her eyes were wide and frightened
and my defiant baby turned meek and obedient.
So I did what a mother must do

when denial is not enough to save a loved one.

I ride in her father's car tonight
in the glare of the ambulance.
Through its back window I see her smiling
chattering away with her escorts
and I feel good and in control
because I have done the right thing
and stared my fears in the face
when I'd rather pretend she was fine.

The night is cool and breezy.
Streetlights twinkle at tourists by the beach.
I tell my friend on the phone,
"It's all right, she's smiling.
We're doing thirty-five, no lights or traffic."
I've been brave, smart, responsible.
I'm in control of my life and my baby's.
My seventeen-year-old fifth baby.

I am enjoying this ride
until the lights start flashing
and the sirens launch their crying
and the eye of the red carriage is shut
and I cannot see my baby's smile anymore
and I have to push seventy
to keep up with the screaming vehicle
where my baby's dying.

"Oh God, oh God, oh God!"
I scream a desperate prayer:
"Please don't let this happen
while her daddy's away
taking care of sick people
in a faraway land without phones or pagers
because I promised him in anger
nothing would happen to her on my watch.
Please, please, please, God!"

I pray and scream in terror
at seventy miles an hour
this sweet and breezy night,
the second of our three-night vacation.
Then the lights go off,
the ambulance slows down
and looks at me again.

Someone flashes me the OK sign.
"It's easy for you to say it's OK
when you're standing next to someone
you never carried inside of you
and never fed with your own life
and can see there is still life in her body.
But I can't see her smiling
and talking to you."

I can only see her, my baby,
wet hair and pale cheeks,
slumped on the stairs
as I called for help,
dragging herself down
with the little bit of life still left in her
and no desire to argue
with her mother.

THE LIFESPAN OF A SONG

Warm humid nights in a Guaynabo carport
singing wholeheartedly with my friends
as my boyfriend plays his Spanish guitar.
We sing and sing and sing
until the milkman shows up!

A houseful of friends, children, and relatives
in Orlando celebrating a birthday,
a graduation, a holiday . . . perhaps our love.
My husband plays the piano or the guitar.
I join in the singing after I do the dishes.

Toga night, the last one of the cruise,
my husband drags me to the stage
appropriately dressed in bed sheets.
Terrific stage fright strangles my vocal chords.
Our children are mortified to see me.

A Christmas party at our home,
eleven days after my hysterectomy,
we dance a slow song while my doctor says
I'm his star patient. My birthday
is in four days, but I don't feel like singing.

More parties at home as the years go by.
Better singers take over.
Our little girls sing so sweetly, in perfect key.
No one invites me to join them,
the hostess with the leastest.

I don't sing anymore, not even in the shower.
The years have silenced me.

NEWS OF THE DAY

We were supposed to go out to a dinner theater
tonight, the day before Valentine's Day,
although we'd been living separately
for five months.

At five o'clock you called to cancel and
said you'd come by later that night
to talk with me.
And you did.

You sat in the brown leather recliner,
at the edge of the seat,
and you looked far away in the distance
when you told me you had a lover.

You had started going out together
three weeks after I moved out,
you said, but I didn't believe you.
You had left me much, much earlier.

"I'm going to have to divorce you now,"
I said, with tears in my eyes.
What kind of an example
would I give my daughters otherwise?

My world collapsed when you left that night.
The dog cried with me for days,
and I had to board him for a while.
I'm still not over you.

I Don't Remember the Day

I don't remember the day
I let go of his hand.
Must have been in my twenties
when I thought to myself,
"I can do this.
I've got what it takes.
I am disciplined, truthful, faithful, strong."

Then I blamed him
for running away from me,
for abandoning me,
for his lies and infidelity.
But why should he hang around
if I didn't need him?
Why stick around

for the nitty-gritty, absurd reality
of day-to-day life
with me and our children
when happiness and freedom
were beckoning him
around the corner?

One day I opened my eyes
and realized how far we'd gone
on this journey of mounting life as a wild bull.
Struggling so hard to dominate it.
Being thrown off and getting back on its hind
a million times and one.

We bandaged our cuts,
splinted our broken bones,
mopped up the sweat off our foreheads,
gritted our teeth, and smiled
at the wild and hot beast under our legs.

We both thought, "Yeah, this time I got it!"
How funny!
How ironic and self-important,
the thought of having learned
how to control the angry and suffering animal
that landed us on the floor
again and again.

And then one day it was over.

The deed was done, the beast was slain.
The bloody matador victorious,
surrounded by devastation
with the corpse still warm and sweaty
in the middle of the arena
for all to see and contemplate:

the triumph of survival
and the terrible, devastating loss
of broken promises.

A year later or a lifetime since,
we'll look each other in the eye
and grieve for our lost future
and the love we'll always have for each other,
dead and buried
in the depths of our souls.

ETERNAL LOVE I

I think of you often
with pity and concern
and a bit of anger and disdain

This gnarled love
unrequited
betrayed

is part of me
like a stone embedded in a tree trunk
after many years, many storms

ETERNAL LOVE II

You think of me now and then
with pity and concern
and a bit of anger and disdain

Your shameful, precious love
double-crossing
and unending

born of insecurity and pain
an irritation in your heart
like the pearl grown in the shell

Medianoche (Midnight)

Inspired by the Despondent Poem I Learned in School

"Inspired by the Despondent Poem I Learned in School" refers to
"I Shall Not Care" by Sara Teasdale (1884–1933).

"When I am dead
  and over me bright April" 14 or Easter Sunday
"shakes out her rain-drenched hair"
  as you wait in vain for my resurrection,
  I shall stay dead.

"When I am dead
  and over me" the lilies bloom in glory
  and your day is filled with gloom,
"Tho' you should lean above me broken-hearted,"
  I will not know.

"I shall have peace,
 as leafy trees are peaceful
when rain bends down the bough,"
and though your tears soak the dirt above me,
I will not grow.

I shall have the peace
that I have so long deserved
after loving you so long
and serving you and protecting you
from cares and strife and storms.

When I am dead
 and finally I'm rested
from loneliness, frustrations, and from scorn,
"I shall not care" if your business is successful,
 if your shirts are ironed,
 or your underpants are torn.

"I shall have peace" from your irritation and your epithets
 when you feel your patience gone.
I will not hear your foul moods
 and your blaming,
your bitterness,
your annoyance,
your misery,
 nor your groans.

"When I am dead and over me bright April
 shakes out her rain-drenched hair,
Tho' you should lean above me broken-hearted"
I will not know.

PTSD

The last time I was in this place of heartbreak
was so long ago I can't remember
the day, the place, the setting.

I just know that when they mentioned her name,
your lover's, this morning
I was back here in an instant.

THE LAST ONE

It appears I'll never get over
the last lover my husband had
before we divorced,
a skinny, well-stacked woman
eighteen years our junior.

She makes me angry.
She makes me anxious.
Her existence ruins
a perfectly good day
and I hate myself for letting it.

As a matter of fact, it's not her
that I grieve about or fear.
It's the memories of the painful relationship
I endured for thirty-seven years
because I didn't know myself.

AN OLD MOOR MAKES A BAD CHRISTIAN

"An old Moor makes a bad Christian,"
we heard a million times growing up,
and I don't know after all these years that
I'll ever make a good ex-wife.

It doesn't really matter now.
It's really OK, I think,
in spite of your longtime lover
and the fact that we keep a proper distance
from one another
since we're still good friends and we'll always be
because we're civilized people
addicted to each other.

Every so often I bury your memory
deep, deep down
where I can't find it
and think, "Now it's gone for good,"
but it's not.

It lives in the dark and humid place
where things rot over the years,
where seeds come to die
and birth new life when the sun shines, finally.

I'm afraid I'm too old
to stop loving you.

ALONE IN A FOREIGN COUNTRY

A modest space with white walls
in a borrowed apartment in Spain.
Brilliant day beyond the window.

Deep inside me, darkness.
There's no one to turn to.

A heart is wrecked.
A marriage has collapsed.
Truly, existentially alone.

An air conditioner whines
in unison
with my physical and emotional
disintegration.

84

Confusion   Anxiety
          overpowering Crying
breathless Bawling
          Weeping   Wailing
Howling   Sobbing

Throat   closes.
Can't   breathe.
          Outside the window
Death   grins   patiently.

Must   call   him,
tell   him
to get me help or I'll
die   here   alone.

His solution?
          Cross the ocean
to enjoy an event
          with his lover present
and profess to the world
          happiness, pleasure, harmony!

Ten years later
it's a certainty:

    this, This, T H I S

Will. Never. Happen.

To Me.   Again!

ALBORADA
(DAWN)

MY NEW OFFICE

It is here, between these four walls,
that I sit and pour my heart out
on a blank page with blinking cursor.

It is here, in this oversized closet,
that I've built a refuge big enough
to store my memories and my efforts

at starting a new life at age sixty.
But inside my heart, as I write,
there are no walls, no boundaries.

The experience is specific
but what I write is universal:
love, heartbreak, regeneration.

SELF-HELP

One, get out of bed:
major accomplishment.

Two, get cleaned and fed;
feed and walk the dog.

Three, get organized:
check To-Do list.

Four, do something productive:
see therapist,
exercise,
get a massage,
buy groceries,
pick up meds,
babysit a grandchild,
write a poem,
water the plants,
vacuum,
do the dishes,
clean the toilet,
post a protest link on Facebook,
call someone who's lonely,
meditate,
whatever . . .

Five, do something foolish:
laugh at self,
take a risk,
call ex-husband's girlfriend—
tell her you want to get along
without mentioning she dated him
while there was a ring
on his left finger.

Six, be grateful,
give someone a hand,
hug someone passionately,
laugh like crazy.

Seven, sleep like a baby.

Eight, repeat.

THE OTHER ME

The other me
suffers from selective amnesia.
She doesn't remember a previous love
or heartbreak.

She flies carefree through life
kissing babies, chatting up strangers,
creating love and happiness
for everyone.

Could I be her?

RESPONSE TO A STATEMENT

"You're very brave to be here,"
my daughters said to me
when I showed up
at the birthday party
where my ex-husband and his lover
sat quietly in a corner.

"I almost chickened out."
"But you made it. That's what counts."

I did. It does.

SURPRISE!

If you had seen me last year
when I reached rock bottom
and gave up on everything and everyone,
you would have thought
there was no way I would get to this point
in less than a year.

But I have, surprise!
And no thanks to you, either.
I worked hard to heal the traumas
of our life together
and to rewire the wrong-thinking brain
I inherited.

I put myself out in the world,
took risks, dared to thrive and lead.
I sat down to write my mother's memories
(scary thoughts of sins
and struggles for perfection)
and I did it.

I even kissed you and your lover, sweetly.

RETORT

"It appears I'll never get over
the latest lover my husband had
before we divorced,"
I wrote not even a month ago.

But there's hope now that I will
because I saw them sitting next to each other,
clinging to each other
in the corner of a room
at a family gathering yesterday
and they seemed so little and scared
as if she was hanging out with her grandfather
and was afraid he'd die in her arms.

That is not the man I fell in love with,
the man I married,
the father of my five children,
the man I went on medical missions with,
and traveled with and had great parties with.
Not even the man who betrayed me many times
or the man I left when I gave up on him.

That was a different man.
I am a different woman.

MY NAILS ARE GROWING NOW

My nails are growing now, my dear,
my hair's not falling out.
My skin is peachy clear and soft, dear,
and I don't even weigh as much
as when you and I were wedded, sweetheart,
and my days were yours alone.

There are no swelling hands and feet, dear,
no more aching of my joints.
I have a sassy brand-new hairdo
and look much cuter than before
when all I pondered was your worries
and how to make you love me more.

It's taken years and tears, *querido*,
and patient people far and near,
yet my children love me, sweetheart.
Their blissful babies kiss me lots.
Now I'm free to be my own self—
full of joy, fulfilled, and whole.

My doggie licks my feet, my darling.
Flowers bloom in bright clay pots.
My piano sings in deep, clear notes now;
fantastic friends enrich my life.
Though I may miss the love I hoped for,
I dream new dreams at night.

I am a brand-new soul now, darling
—a brand-new soul I am.

FORGET WHAT I
SAID EARLIER

Some time ago, when I was still hurting,
I said I was not over you.
I spoke it in despair and loneliness,
plus romantic notions of what could have been.

But then something turned around
and I saw your young lover
hopefully putting up for a few years
what I put up with for almost forty

with the same hope and will
but with much less tolerance.
I saw myself in her mirror
and she saw herself in mine.

She pretended she was fearless.
I smiled to myself:
"For how long?"
We kissed goodbye like good friends.

I went home to live a full life
and, without lifting a finger,
found attraction, joy, and welcome
in new eyes that looked deeply into mine.

I'll always care about you,
I know quite clearly now,
but I am so, so over you
because I love me more.

VALENTINE FOR AN OLD WOMAN WITH NEW ROOMMATES

It used to be too serene in here.
Days crawled along
leaving a silvery, slippery trace
of lonely tears and drudgery.

A little brown angel of destruction and energy
bursts into my home one day,
all mischievous giggles and twinkling eyes.
His big black dog of soulful eyes tags along
as his grieving mother starts over.

The anxiety of love—ancient, slow, shattered love—
opens a path among misplaced furniture
and traces of an office sundered and dispersed
for his homeless family.

Horrific screams
test the timbre of his voice and our stamina.
Little cars fly through space,
mindless of treasured mementos.

My aged pet growls at the new dog's goading.
Chaos. Mayhem. Panic.
Dogs go berserk over the child's boundless vitality.

His mother's spirit shakes, eyes brim with tears.
My throat locks, heart thumps, chest tightens.

I crave a discreet place
to disguise my distress
rediscover my essence
salvage my chutzpah.

Now, a chocolate cherub wants to cuddle his Awa.
Wraps his arms 'round my neck
and mumbles he loves me—
a precious burden that pleases my soul.

Sloppy wet kisses comfort old cheeks
with the progress we're making,
dogs at our feet and his sweet momma smiling.

I CAN SING!!!

It had been a long day
going back and forth
from meeting to meeting,
working out all the kinks in the process
of surgically removing my husband
of thirty-eight years from my life.

I'd endured the high heels,
the Florida heat,
the difficult negotiations,
almost running out of gas
in the course of getting lost
and finding my way again.

I managed to cry only two tears
and smile throughout the day.
My therapist, as proud as a mother
or an artist almost finished with her sculpture,
thought I was healing
well enough on my own.

Mind you,
I have a deep, wide scar
in my chest
where my childhood prince,
my Siamese twin
used to be.

But I am proud of my accomplishments:
I have taken care of my needs
with elegance, humanity, sophistication.

100

I give myself a standing ovation
complete with bouquets of flowers
and cheers from the full house of life.

I get ready for the Neighborhood Fiesta
where I arrive fashionably late
in turquoise heels and low neckline.
I look good. I feel good.
I love the live music,
and the music loves me.

I sing along loud and clear
tune after tune after delicious, nourishing tune.
My blood is pumping,
my face is shining—
my song gives pleasure to the old guitar
looking for a soul mate.

I laugh soundlessly at the old little me
who believed that I just couldn't sing
as well as my ex
and stopped singing
for more than forty years
except to my babies.

I'm invited to another performance
some other day in a different world,
and I know I will go
with or without high heels
or a sexy dress
or a companion for protection.

I can take care of myself.
I am Strong
    Beautiful
    Brave
and I Can Sing!!!

ODE TO MY CHICKEES

I look at my children gathered around me,
my *pollitos*, my chickees,
and my soul inhales the sweetness
of their innate love for me.

It hasn't changed in quality since they were little,
but now it's fully feathered, mature,
having birthed little ones of their own
or cuddled their siblings' offspring.

Why would I choose among them,
my darlings, the beautiful miracles
whose tiny toes I kissed,
young souls I bathed and protected?

I wasn't the perfect mother.
They were never perfect children.
We drove each other nuts on occasion
and sometimes communication faltered.

I laughed when they yelled,
"I hate you, Mami!"
because they didn't like my rules
or boundaries.

I cried each first day of school,
each baptism, illness, graduation,
wrestling my own self to let them fly away
and risk failure and heartbreak.

I look now at my *pollitos* around me
and their spouses and sweethearts, my beloved.
They worried and fretted about me
when I lost parents, husband, brothers.

I see pride in their eyes now, mostly,
as they break free of the shells that constrain them
and find hope to peck at their own dreams
in my rebirth, novel life, radiant daybreak.

ACKNOWLEDGMENTS

For the First Edition

To my six grandchildren, who have given me life and inspiration when I most needed it. And to the rest of *mis pollitos,* my chickees, who continue to encourage and love me no matter what. You are my inspiration, my deepest and purest loves!

To my writers' critique group members—Bettie Wailes, Doug Grossman, Frances Ellen, and Teresa TL Bruce—who convinced me I was a writer and obliged me by critiquing my poetry when we were supposed to be working on fiction.

To my editor, Teresa TL Bruce (https://TealAshes.com/), who polished and organized this collection until it was so beautiful and made so much sense that it made me cry the first time I read it out loud. Her many talents and generous encouragement made this book come to light.

To my proofreader, Marsha Butler (SwmpWriter@gmail.com), who graciously made time to make sure there were no last-minute mistakes. A big thank-you for saying yes when I needed you. You saved the day!

To my beta readers—Deborah Kristal, Susan Gurnik, Sylvia Rojas-Vaughn (https://DallasPoetsCom.org/index.html), Vivienne Martin, Ann Brown, Tony Burnett (http://WritersLeagueOfTexas.wordpress.com/), Coralis Solomon, Stephani Ceballos, T.K. Thorne (https://TKThorne.com/), Alice Friedman, Elaine Person (www.PersonalWrite.com), Mona Frazier (http://AlvaradoFrazier.com), Armando Rendón (https://www.SomosEnEscrito.

com/), Jan Schomp, Nancy Reil Rojas (https://www.EbooksByNancy.com/), Javier Mora Hayes, Oscar Peña, and Adele Phillips. My work is richer and more appealing because of your critiques. Thanks for your generosity and insights. I love you all!

To Misfit Creative (https://TinyURL.com/misfitcreative, formerly najcreatives) for a beautiful and outstanding cover and for challenging me to do the artwork myself. Your patience, commitment to the quality of this work, and creativity in designing the layout paid off with an award-winning cover I am proud of.

To Lisbet Photography (http://www.LisbetStudio.com/) for a beautiful collection of author pictures and for making me feel happy and relaxed while taking them.

To my ex-husband, without whose financial support I would not have had the time and energy to work on this book. Thank you for supporting this project and encouraging me along.

To Writer's Digest's Robert Lee Brewer, whose 2013 November Chapbook Challenge prompts reminded me I could still write poetry after all those years and thus inspired me to more than double the size of this collection.

For the Second Edition

So much time has passed since I admitted I was a poet and decided to share my work with the world! I had five grandchildren at the time and now have six, my dog Pillín died, and I have a new puppy, Canela (Nela for short). I acquired new skills, read a ton of books, wrestled with my health and recovered, and built a wider and stronger network of friends, professional collaborators, and readers.

One thing that hasn't changed is the love and support I have received from my family members, each in their own special way, as I struggled to overcome obstacles of all kinds. My talented photographer/daughter, Nylda Beatriz Aldarondo-Jeffries (https://TinyURL.com/misfitcreative) put special effort into producing an author's picture that reflects my nature. Her cover design for the first edition of this book received an International Latino Book Award. Her son, my beloved Kai Aldarondo-Jeffries, whose technical expertise rescues me every time I get bogged down with my website or newsletter, belies his youth. His graphic arts talents helped me with the design of my logo and business card. And my ex-husband's continued support as a father of our children, friend, and financial supporter is something else I am grateful for.

Other things have also stayed constant like the gracious help of my beta readers, readers and writers alike—Mercedita Arias, Sandra Crawford, Kathy Cressey, Charlene Edge, Juliana Aragón Fatula, Jacqueline Klappenbach, Ken Pelham, Elaine Person, Lynn Schiffhorst, and T. K. Thorne—who took the time to read and critique my work, some of them to an exquisite level of detail.

The Writers Hotel editors Shanna McNair and Scott Wolven provided great feedback on the new poems included in this edition and many others for an upcoming book. Their praise and encouragement and the opportunity to work and learn with the TWH participants and faculty throughout the years have nurtured my growth as a poet and writer.

My faithful and talented editor, Teresa TL Bruce, deserves special mention for agreeing to edit this second edition without flinching at the errors that, through no fault of her own, were left in the first edition. She rigorously and painstakingly reviewed each word, character, and space of my work and suggested changes to ensure a gratifying reading experience and the transmission of the ideas and emotions that I was somehow failing to convey. Without Teresa's kind encouragement, one new poem that has such an enormous impact on the quality of this collection, "The Lifespan of a Song," would not have been born. She has given birth to this book as much as I have! (She has earned one of my precious exclamation points— and these too!!!)

I must acknowledge the brilliant creative talent of Sanja Mosic at Blacklady Design for her professionalism and kind support as I struggled to communicate the ideas I wanted my book to convey. Autumn Skye's inspired interpretation of Sanja's work has truly made this poetic memoir a work of art.

It has been a great pleasure to work with Arielle Haughee and the staff of Orange Blossom Publications. We collaborated quite cheerfully and efficiently on every step of the book design, publication, and marketing—from creating a new title for this edition (with Teresa Bruce's help) to preparing for a successful book launch and every step in between. I am proud of your work and professionalism, Arielle!

LISTS OF NEW AND REVISED POEMS

S ince I endorse an open and transparent lifestyle, I think it's a good
idea to inform readers of my new and newly revised poems. The titles
below are grouped first with an explanation of each category and then by
the order of their appearance in this book.

Brand-New Poems

These poems were newly birthed for this second edition of *Alborada (Dawn): A
Cross-Cultural Memoir in Poetry*.

Trigger Warning
Growth Song
First Crush
Memories of a Portrait en Plein Air
Wishes in the Wind
Realization II
To the Young Woman in the Old Photo
A Tiny Thing Makes All the Difference
About Life
The Lifespan of a Song
Eternal Love I
Eternal Love II
Alone in a Foreign Country
Valentine for an Old Woman with New Roommates

NYLDA DIEPPA

Revised Poems

These poems from the first edition of *Alborada* underwent thoughtful revision for this new edition. While essentially the same poems as their previously published namesakes, each has evolved with subtle—or not so subtle—reviving transformations.

> A Secret Message
> Sheet Music
> In Love Again
> Impossibles
> Always in My Heart
> Prudence
> Vacation
> Inspired by the Despondent Poem I Learned in School
> I Can Sing!!!
> Ode to My Chickees

Foundational Poems

These poems connect the core of the old and new editions of *Alborada (Dawn)* as they appear virtually unchanged in this edition (except for minor stylistic adjustments to capitalization and punctuation).

> Love Poem
> Reinita
> Binocular
> Lineage
> Nanileiloe
> The Element
> Another Name fore Dedication
> On How I Want to Write
> Something Sweet
> Realization
> Flying High
> Exploration
> Damn Free
> Halfway Point

Slow Sunset in Sarasota
Pineapple Flight
Ode to the Gravid Banana Tree
Love Song in Two Tempos
Nuera
News of the Day
I Don't Remember the Day
PTSD
The Last One
An Old Moor Makes a Bad Christian
My New Office
Self-Help
The Other Me
Response to a Statement
Surprise!
Retort
My Nails Are Growing Now
Forget What I Said Earlier

Upcoming Titles from this Author

Otra Alborada: Wisdom Emerges with the New Dawn, a new collection of poems illustrating lessons learned from love and loss

Alborada: Una memoria intercultural en poesía, a translation into Spanish of *Alborada (Dawn): A Poetic Memoir Across Cultures*

Amada, a novel set in Puerto Rico and Florida, based on miracles that shaped the life of the author's mother

ABOUT THE AUTHOR

Image by Nylda Beatriz Photography
https://TinyURL.com/misfitcreative

Nylda Dieppa is a speaker, author, facilitator, translator, and LGBTQ+ supporter and ally enjoying life in Florida. Her work has been published in various publications including *America Magazine*, the *Florida Catholic*, *Somos en escrito* magazine, *La Respuesta* magazine, and *Cadence*. Nylda is currently revising *Amada*, a novel based on the life of her mother in Puerto Rico and Florida.

For more information, visit Nylda's website at NyldaDieppa.com and sign up to receive her inspirational "Word Sketches" newsletter.

CPSIA information can be obtained
at www.ICGtesting.com
Printed in the USA
JSHW080023020523
41120JS00001B/79